Anonymous

The Velocipede

Its History, Varieties, and Practice

Anonymous

The Velocipede
Its History, Varieties, and Practice

ISBN/EAN: 9783337200817

Printed in Europe, USA, Canada, Australia, Japan

Cover: Foto ©Andreas Hilbeck / pixelio.de

More available books at **www.hansebooks.com**

THE

VELOCIPEDE;

ITS

HISTORY, VARIETIES, AND PRACTICE

WITH ILLUSTRATIONS.

NEW YORK:
PUBLISHED BY HURD AND HOUGHTON.
Cambridge: Riverside Press.
1869.

RIVERSIDE, CAMBRIDGE:

STEREOTYPED AND PRINTED BY

H. O. HOUGHTON AND COMPANY.

PREFACE.

WHEN the rumor first came across the water, a few years ago, of that wonderful and fascinating little two-wheeled machine, upon which one could so gracefully annihilate time and space, the author of this little book was seized with his first attack of Velocipede Fever.

When, in the spring of 1868, we heard how popular this invention was becoming in France, how much it was ridden in Paris; in its Boulevards, its Bois de Boulogne, and on the smooth paths of the Champs Elysées; how it was employed for amusement in the Garden of the Tuileries, and by the laborer in the suburbs going to his daily toil; how exhilarating to the gentleman, how useful to the messenger and post-boy, we were again seized with the disease with renewed virulence.

We could hardly delay for one from across the Atlantic, and embraced the first opportunity to learn the art of riding. While learning, with bruised elbows and scraped knees, with the bicycle more of the time on us than we on it, we felt how usefully

we could employ a few hints of instruction, and how
invaluable we should find some little book that would
tell us all about the machine.

After we were somewhat proficient, we were
amazed that we had not learned before, and saw
how easily we could have done so, if we had only
been a little informed of the method of procedure.

When we proposed purchasing, we were all adrift,
as likely to buy a poor machine as a good one, and
anxiously scanned the papers, and inquired of friends
concerning the merits and demerits of each patent
and make.

So far as we can learn, there has been no book
written upon the Velocipede, either abroad or in this
country.

It is the design of this little work, not only to give
a few simple directions to guide the beginner, but to
give the history of the machine from its first origin,
to treat accurately and impartially of the strength,
lightness, superiority, and inferiority of each important machine and patent, and to collect such facts,
statistics, and items, as may be of use and information to any one interested in the subject.

We think it an invention which will not have an
ephemeral popularity, but which will, in its way, rev-
olutionize travel for all time. We love the velocipede, and can truly quote, " Amor jussit scribere."

We wish to thank the various manufacturers for

their kindness in giving us information, and to acknowledge our indebtedness to various newspapers that have fallen in our way, to the " Scientific American," to the " Galaxy," and to the " Velocipedist," and its genial and accomplished young editor.

CAMBRIDGE, *March* 20, 1869.

CONTENTS.

THE VELOCIPEDE:

ITS HISTORY AND ORIGIN.

———◆———

WE have spent much time in fruitless and weary researches over old French books and musty journals, and have found that there is but very little about the Velocipede, in the literature, or dictionaries and encyclopedias of ancient or modern times.

In the " Journal de Paris " of July 27, 1779, there is a description of a vehicle invented by Messrs. Blanchard and Mesurier, the former the celebrated aeronaut, which was exhibited on the Place Louis XV., named to-day Place de Concorde, in the presence of many members of the French Academy and a large concourse of spectators. At the head of the machine was the figure of an eagle, with outspread wings, to which was attached the apparatus with which the driver directed its movements. Behind it was seated an individual who propelled the machine. At a subsequent date, the inventor transported the vehicle to Versailles, and exhibited its capabilities, in the presence of Louis XVI., Marie Antoinette, and their effeminate court.

At a later date M. Dreuze made an improvement
on this invention, which met with some success as a
toy. A number of these machines were constructed
after his model, and distributed among country postmen, who used the novelty for a time, until a heavy
fall of snow rendered them unserviceable, when they
were abandoned, greatly to the gratification of a con-
servative class, who, detesting anything in the way
of innovation, had prophesied their failure.

The article upon the Velocipede in the " American
Encyclopedia," commences by giving the well-known
derivation of the word from the Latin *velox*, swift,
and *pes*, a foot, and defines it as a carriage, by means
of which the rider propels himself along the ground,
and states that it was invented at Manheim.

In a little old French book called " Dictionnaire
de Conversation," under the word *Velocipede*, we
are referred to the word *Drasienne*, on turning to
which, we find a description of the three-wheeled
arm movement Velocipede, and the credit of its invention ascribed to Baron Charles Drais de Saverbrun, at Manheim, at the early commencement of the
nineteenth century. The Drasienne, though a decidedly crude idea, differed very materially from the
clumsy structure of Messrs. Blanchard and Mesurier.

Baron Drais de Saverbrun seems to be universally
considered the inventor of the germ, which has developed into the present improved Velocipede. He

was a man of considerable scientific attainments, and author of several works; son of a lawyer, himself a landscape gardener; and died at Carlsruhe, December 12, 1851. He was master of the woods and forests of the Grand Duke of Baden, and rode about upon the Drasienne, while performing his official duties.

This invention made its *début* in 1816, in the garden of Tivoli, which was at that time the favorite resort of the *crême de la crême* of Parisian society. As originally constructed it appears to have been of the most simple kind. It consisted of a bar five feet long, supported at each end upon a single wheel, that designed for the front being so arranged as to turn obliquely to the line of the carriage. The rider sat astride the bar, and propelled the machine by the action of the feet upon the ground. The motion was much like walking upon the heels; as the feet were brought down flat, the heels were the first to touch. The vehicle was never generally patronized, because the pleasure of riding it was counterbalanced by the labor of propelling it. It was called the " Célérifère," or " makespeed," and many shafts of ridicule were leveled mercilessly at it. The mode of propelling it was not graceful, and this ridicule was not without foundation. It disappeared from view in France almost as rapidly as its inventor expected it to roll into public favor.

This novel vehicle, under the name of " Drasina " was introduced into England in 1818, and, at first, the greatest possible expectations were created, with regard to its usefulness and speed. It was maintained, that it would travel up-hill on a post-road as fast as a man could walk ; that on a level, even after a heavy rain, it would average six or seven miles an hour; and that, on a descent, it would equal a horse at full speed. It was described in the advertisements of the day as " consisting of two wheels, one behind the other, connected by a perch, on which a saddle is placed as a seat. The front wheel is made to turn on a pivot, guided by a circular lever or rudder, which comes up to the hand ; *the fore-arms rest on a cushion in front;* in this position, both hands holding the rudder firmly, the machine and traveller are preserved *in equilibrio.*

In 1821 Lewis Gompertz of Surrey, introduced some decided improvements upon the Drasina, as will be seen from the accompanying engraving, extracted from the 39th volume of the English " Repertory of Arts."

The object of the improvement of Gompertz was to bring the arms of the rider into action, in assistance to his legs. It consisted " in the application of a handle, C, which is to be worked backwards and forwards, to which is attached a circular rack, D G, which works in a pinion, E, with ratch wheel on the front wheel of the velocipede, and which, on being pulled by the rider with both hands, sends the machine forward; and when thrust from him does not send it back again, on account of the ratch, which allows the pinion to turn in that direction, free of the wheel. H is the saddle, and the rest, B is so made that the breast of the rider bears against it, while the

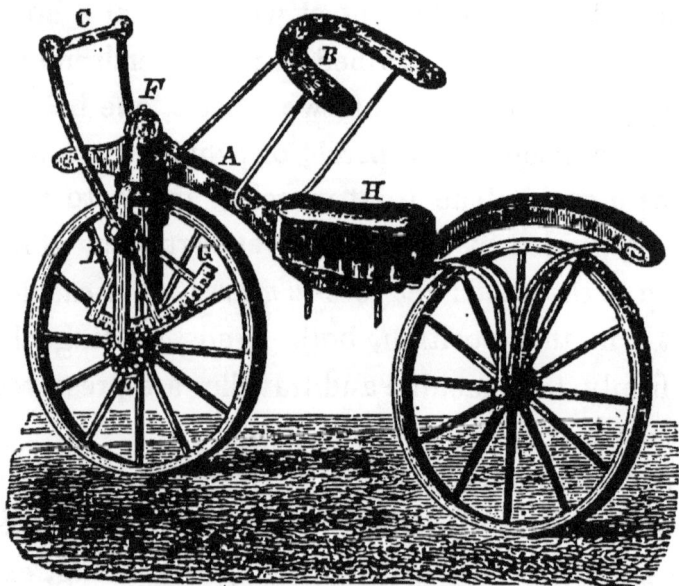

sides come around him at some distance below the arms, and is stuffed." The rider could with this machine either propel it entirely without the feet, or he could use the feet, while the arms were free. The beam, A, was made of beech wood, and a pivot at F, allowed the front wheel to be turned to the right or left at the will of the rider. This must have been, although somewhat clumsily shaped, quite an effi-

cient machine, good for the times — forty-eight years
ago. It will be seen that it has many features
in common with the one now in vogue, though the
difference in the manner of propelling completely
changes the character of the vehicle.

Among those who distinguished themselves on the
velocipede in England was Michael Faraday the
chemist, who frequently drove his machine through
the suburbs of London.

The velocipede was cultivated most assiduously
for some little time by the sporting gentry of England; but Lord George Bentinck and other persons
of fashion finally pronounced so decidedly against it,
that it descended to the vulgar level of a plaything
for young people, and ceased to be regarded in any
other light than that of a toy or hobby. While the
fever lasted, a shoemaker of London made much
money by the manufacture of a strong shoe, soled
with iron, which greatly aided the feet of the " Ve-
locipeders," as they went over the ground.

William Howitt, in his " Visits to Remarkable
Places," a book published in 1841, makes mention
of the velocipede as follows — the passage is taken
from a description of Alnwick Castle, the ancient seat
of the Percy family : " Among the curiosities laid up
here, are also two velocipedes, machines which twenty
years ago were for a short period much in vogue.
One young man of my acquaintance rode on one of

these wooden horses all the way from London to Falkirk in Scotland, and was requested at various towns to exhibit his management of it to the ladies and gentlemen of the place. He afterward made a long excursion to France upon it. He was a very adroit velocipedean, and was very much amused with the circumstance of a gentleman meeting him by the river side, who, requesting to be allowed to try it, and being shown how he must turn the handle in order to guide it, set off with great spirit, but turning the wrong way, soon found himself hurrying to the edge of the river, where in his flurry, instead of turning the handle the other way, he began lustily shouting ' Woh!' ' woh!' and so crying plunged headlong into the stream. The Duke's horse, which is laid up here for the gratification of posterity, was, I believe, not so unruly ; yet I was told its pranks caused it to be disused and here stabled. It is said that the duke and his physicians used to amuse themselves with careering about the grounds on these steeds ; but one day being somewhere on the terrace, his grace's Trojan steed capsized, and rolled over and over with him down the green bank, much to the amusement of a troop of urchins who were mounted on a wall by the road to witness this novel kind of racing. On this accident the velocipede was laid up in lavender, and a fine specimen of the breed it is. I asked the old porter if the story was true, but he only said, ' Mind!

I did not tell you that. Don't pretend to say, if you write any account of this place, that you had that from me.' "

The machine was introduced into New York in 1819, where it was given the English name of " Hobby-horse " or " Dandy-horse." The excitable citizens went into an ecstasy of astonishment and delight, and the manufacturers found it impossible to meet the demand. A place was opened for their exhibition near Bowling Green, and people used to run on them up and down the Bowery, and the hill that led from Chatham Street to the City Hall Park. The' rage for them soon extended throughout the country ; and we hear of them in Philadelphia, Yonkers, Troy, Saratoga, and Boston. At Troy in the fall of 1819, a firm, Davis and Rogers, manufactured a number of machines, and used to let them to the young bloods about town, at twenty-five cents an hour. In Boston they became quite common, and, moonlight nights, students from the classic shades of Old Harvard could be seen running them across the long bridge into the city.

In a New York paper of those days we find an interesting account of a newly invented velocipede for ladies then building " by a distinguished artist." " It is to have beams, or bodies on springs, and four wheels which will insure its safety. It is to quarter on the road like other carriages ; and with four *impe*-

lers it is supposed it will proceed with astonishing rapidity; but its peculiar recommendation is to be conveyance of two ladies and two *impellers* at the rate of six miles an hour."

The " Ladies Literary Cabinet" (published corner Chatham and Duane streets), of Saturday, August 9, 1819, gives a very amusing account of a hoax which seems to have completely deceived the citizens: " VELOCIPEDE HOAX. Some mischievous wag on Saturday last, caused printed hand-bills to be distributed, announcing that on Monday at five o'clock precisely, a velocipede would start from the head of Chatham Square, and proceed to St. Paul's Church in less than two minutes, and that it would afterward be exhibited in the Park, etc. Notwithstanding the rain on Monday, the people began to collect at an early hour, so that before five o'clock Chatham Street was literally crowded from one end to the other. Every window from the basement to the attic was thrown open, and filled with the beautiful heads of ladies and children, exposed to the incessant searching mist, which robbed their lovely tresses of every curl which the morning's industry had created. But female fortitude and curiosity combined, are not to be shaken by wind and weather. For more than an hour did the throng continue to increase, until it was almost impossible to pass the street with or without a velocipede. In the mean

time, the Park was also crowded, and the City Hall
exhibited the appearance of a gala-day. It is need-
less to say that no velocipede appeared."

Since that time down to a recent day, when M.
Lallement, of France, took it in hand, all experiments to render the machine subservient to practical
purposes appear to have been unsatisfactory, and it
has only been used as a toy, with the modification
of a third wheel. M. Lallement succeeded in affix-
ing to the front wheel of the two-wheeled machine,
treadles which should be acted upon by the feet.
His success attending his endeavors to ride it, was
beyond his most sanguine expectations. After becoming a thorough master of the tandem team, he
appeared upon the Champs Elysees, and created a
genuine *furore*. People not only wondered that
such a strange machine should run so swiftly, but
that it should run at all upon two wheels in a line.
He obtained a patent upon his velocipede, and sold
it to Messrs. Michaux & Co., of Paris, who have
since improved much upon it. M. Lallement, with
James Carroll, of New Haven, Conn., obtained a
patent in this country in 1866.

The machines now in use are so radically different
from those of fifty years ago, so perfect in propelling
power, so easy to ride, so swift of motion, so useful
as a means of conveyance, that it seems impossible
for history to repeat itself with regard to the present
mania.

THE BICYCLE.

Of the various kinds of velocipedes, four, three, two, and one wheeled, the bicycle seems to be considered the most artistic, is altogether the most in favor, and steadily maintains its ground against all rivals. Whether it will be the model velocipede of the future remains to be seen. The various experiments now being tried will, no doubt, eventually result in a nearly perfect machine, but it will require a season's experience fully to develop the ingenuity of our American artisans.

Many have expressed doubts as to the real utility of the velocipede, and the permanency of its use. They seem to think it a frivolous invention only cal- culated to serve purposes of amusement, and soon to be superseded by some other ephemeral claimant for popularity. Most of these have based their opin- ions upon the disuse into which rude machines have fallen in former times. But the difference in the construction of the modern velocipede from the primitive one has entirely changed the character of the vehicle. It is no longer a draft vehicle, but a locomotive, and as much superior.to the original bar on wheels, as the improved steam locomotive is to the old time stage-coach.

We believe in the utility, convenience, and econ- omy of the innovation, as well as in its capacity for affording amusement, and developing strength and skill; and believe as now improved, it is destined to mark an era in the history of vehicles. It has passed the period of being a mere toy, and although as the novelty wears away, there may be less enthu- siasm, it will continue to be used, and in an increas- ing degree, for street locomotion. With those who live in the cities and require a daily exercise, exhilar- ating, pleasant, healthful, and free from expense; with those who reside in the country and have long distances to traverse daily in reaching the scene of their labors, or with those who have leisure and wealth at their command, but love such exercises as afford an opportunity for the display of grace, agility, and skill, the velocipede has already become as great a favorite in this country as it is in France and England.

Its want of adaptability to the roughly paved road-ways of our cities, is already, in a great measure, overcome, and experience has proved its facility *in rure*. We have seen the bicycle run with ease on country roads, and dashing with full speed through city streets, totally regardless of curbstones or crossings. In New York, no matter where you go, a velocipede is sure to whiz past you. The school-boy rides up Fifth Avenue in the morning, with his books strapped before him. In Broadway, where stages, wagons, carts, trucks, and carriages, clog the street from morning till night, the iron steed may be seen gracefully cutting its way among the larger vehicles. The exercise is not tiresome, except to the beginner. We have found twelve miles on a country road no more fatiguing than a brisk walk of two. We believe a man may ride and drive one at the rate of ten miles an hour, with less fatigue than he could walk one quarter of that distance. Some people ride easier than others, as some skate easier. Some people make hard work of anything. Lazy

people will never fall in love with the bicycle, because
to ride one requires all the faculties to be alive and
in action. To keep one's balance, however, does
not require that constant labor and exertion which
novices suppose. "Familiarity breeds contempt,"
the old adage says. Familiarity with the bicycle
becomes a sort of second nature, and a velocipedian,
after a fair amount of experience, finds himself· almost as perfectly at home astride his two-wheeler,
as he does on his feet.

When John Brent rode his horse across the plains
in search of adventure, the era of the two-wheeled
velocipede had ·not come upon us. We think the
bicycle an animal, which will, in a great measure,
supersede the horse. It does not cost as much; it
will not eat, kick, bite, get sick, or die. It requires
no stabling, no feed, no water, no curry-comb. It
never "balks," or "rares up." It never needs a hal-
ter or a harness. It is light, and little, and leans
lovingly against you for support. Its gait is uniform
and easy, beautiful and exhilarating to see, and simple to analyze. It glides along with smooth grace,
as though it were alive.

Young America is pictured coming in on a velocipede. Henry Ward Beecher thinks the coming man
will ride one, and we shall not be surprised to see
his prediction fulfilled, and devout worshippers propelling themselves to church on Sunday with all due
gravity and decorum.

Velocipeding is a hopeful sign of progress. If that man is a benefactor who makes two blades of grass grow where but one grew before, he should come in for a share of praise, who teaches a man to go ten miles as easily and as quickly as he previously went one. "Time is money;" and whatever of it is saved is often so much cash. As the velocipede serves its purpose in this direction, it may be regarded as a good savings institution.

We think that decided good will grow out of this invention. Riding the velocipede affords pleasurable excitement, which is what most men drink liquor for, and it leaves no sting behind. It takes men from the bar-rooms out into the pure air, into God's light and sunshine, and braces their lungs with the very breath of Heaven. It stimulates them to save what they would otherwise spend foolishly, that they may invest it in a machine which is a source of health and pleasure, as well as of utility. It is an inducement to young men who work in close apartments to spend more time in the open air, and furnishes them a means of healthful, invigorating, and, at the same time, pleasant exercise, such as nothing else can possibly afford.

Serious accidents on the velocipede are almost unheard of, and the predictions that these machines would prove dangerous have not been verified. It will fall down, but the rider need not fall with it unless he chooses. It is no more dangerous than a horse and carriage, under any circumstances, and not nearly so much so, with ordinary caution.

The speed attained by the swifter kind of velocipede on the roads, averages from twelve to thirteen miles an hour. On a smooth, level floor, such a speed can be maintained with but little effort on almost any machine. It is safe to say that a good velocipede rider can travel a hundred miles as quickly as an ordinary horse with an ordinary load. Of course, the more a person rides, the easier it becomes, and the less the fatigue.

In impelling a velocipede, the limbs are not constantly in motion; for on level ground, when the impetus is at the average rate, or when the machine is descending an incline, the feet may be removed from the pedals, and the legs be placed on the bar, fixed in front of the machine for that purpose. A slight impulsion to the vehicle from time to time suffices to keep up the speed. When a rider encounters a formidable hill, he can dismount and lead his bicycle by the hand. He can do this with almost the same ease that he can carry an ordinary walking-stick. A hill, to be insurmountable, has to be, however, of more than average steepness. Though Massachusetts is proverbially hilly, there is no ascent between Boston and Worcester, a distance of thirty miles, that cannot be ridden over with the bicycle.

The best speed thus far attained on the road is a mile in a few seconds over three minutes. A gentleman in New Jersey, a few weeks since, travelled fifty miles in four hours and a half. A gentleman residing in 22d Street, New York, goes down town to his business on his velocipede in twelve minutes. Adepts abroad find no difficulty whatever in accomplishing fully fifty miles in five hours, without once alighting from their vehicles. A few months ago, a couple of amateurs, making a tour through a part of France, challenged each other as to which could perform the greatest distance in four and twenty hours. One accomplished eighty-seven miles, the other one hundred and twenty-three. A party of nine quitted Rouen early in the morning on their velocipedes, and arrived in Paris in time for dinner the same evening; having performed the distance of eighty-five miles, exclusive of stoppages, and at a rate of speed averaging between ten and twelve miles an hour. An English gentleman travelled the distance from London to Bristol, one hundred and thirty-five miles, between the hours of three o'clock, P. M., one day, and ten A. M. the next, stopping some hours in Reading.

In Paris, the Americans carry off the prizes for slow as well as fast riding. The slow riding is much the more difficult. It is much easier for the rider to keep his equilibrium while riding swiftly.

Dr. Oliver Wendell Holmes once published an article in the " Atlantic Monthly," entitled " The Human Wheel; its Spokes and Felloes ; " in which he treated the act of walking as analagous to the movement of a wheel: the legs being the spokes and the feet the felloes. Had he postponed his humorous and instructive essay a year or two, he would have found himself behind the age.

It is perhaps not generally known to what an extent the bicycle mania prevails, and how rapidly the idea has germinated, budded, and bloomed, not only throughout our own country, but in various parts of the world. In New York some ten thousand pupils are ready to graduate from the schools and appear upon the roads. In Boston there will soon be nearly as many more; while Philadelphia, Chicago, St. Louis, and San Francisco count their experts by the hundred and their novices by the thousand. We hear of the bicycle in the far West and in Texas. We read that New Orleans proposes to purchase velocipedes for its fire companies, and hear of a velocipede military company in Louisville. We play velocipede music, and in our walks velocipede ". Livery Stables " and " Velocipedes to Let," greet our eyes. The shop-windows on our fashionable thoroughfares display Velocipede Hats, Velocipede Gloves, and Velocipede Shoes.

The machines have become so numerous on the

sidewalks of Providence, New Bedford, and other
New England towns, that the stunned authorities
contemplated prohibiting their use, as a nuisance.
The various merits of various machines are dis-
cussed on the street corners with as much zeal as
were ever the diversified merits of horse-flesh; and.
experts are to be heard talking of these new substi-
tutes for legs as jockeys are wont to talk of the
wind, strength, bottom, gait, and "go" of Eclipses,
Dexters, and Ethan Allens.

In France, fashion writers and fashion leaders
rack their brains for the contrivance of .velocipede
costumes; velocipede clubs are formed; velocipede
championships contested for at velocipede tournaments. There are not less than ten thousand
machines running in the streets of Paris. They are
used by postmen, government employees, students,
messengers, and peddlers; and shopmen send their
clerks about on machines covered with flashy advertisements. All velocipedes there are required to carry
lanterns in the evening, and though we have no such
regulations here, young gentlemen may be seen almost every night, in our cities, riding their velocipedes with head-lights attached.

In Paris they can be seen driving at break-neck
speed along the narrow stone parapet beside the
Seine, and even down the hundred steps of the Tro-
cadéro, their riders all the time indulging in gymnastic

feats that would seem to invite certain destruction. ·At Rome, gentlemen practice the bicycle in the court-yards, and are seen riding on the Piazza de Spagna. Country trips are taken upon them in Japan, and they are no longer a novelty in the streets of the larger Chinese cities.

PATENTS AND THE RIGHTS OF MANU-FACTURERS.

———◆———

EARLY in last winter, a great rivalry began to develop itself in the business of manufacturing velocipedes; and the demand became so large, as to lead the principal carriage-makers of the country into making it an important branch of their business. At that time it was generally understood that any manufacturer was at liberty to make the two-wheeled velocipede, in any way he deemed most profitable.

When the *furore* first manifested itself, Mr. Calvin Witty of Broadway, New York, saw it would be a "big thing," and very quietly went to work to find out in what way the business of making the machine could be controlled. He ascertained, by careful investigation, that a patent had been recorded, covering the principal features of the bicycle, now in such popular use. He sought out the owners of the patent, found them in moderate circumstances, eager to turn to account rights which had heretofore been of but little avail, and purchased of them for a comparatively small sum. He now claims to hold the right to the exclusive use of the two-wheeled velocipede, with treadle and guiding arms. This patent, however, does not cover the idea of making a two-wheeled machine, or of applying a propelling power.

As soon as Mr. Witty had completed his arrangements, he ascertained the names of parties engaged in manufacturing velocipedes throughout the country, and the majority of them were the astonished recipients of the following notification : —

"No. 638 BROADWAY, N. Y., *Feb.* 3*d*, 1869.

"You are hereby notified, that Letter Patent No. 59,915, granted Nov. 20th, 1866, secures a velocipede with the two wheels, treadle, and guiding arms; and that the velocipede you are manufacturing is an infringement upon said patent. The present is to require you to cease the further manufacture of said velocipede, and to settle with me for all past infringements of the rights under said patent.

(Signed)   "CALVIN WITTY."

The following is a copy of the record of the patent, registered at the Patent Office in Washington :—

"Patent No. 59,915. Pierre Lallement, Paris, France, assignor to himself and James Carroll, New Haven, Conn. Velocipede. Nov. 20th, 1866.

"The fore wheel is axled in the jaws of a depending bar which is riveted in the frame, and turned by a horizontal lever bar. This wheel is revolved by a treadle crank.

Claim: The combination and arrangement of the two wheels, provided with the treadles and the guiding arms, so as to operate substantially, and for the purpose herein set forth."

Some manufacturers were nonplused by Mr. Witty's warning, and stopped their work entirely. Others paid no attention to the demand, considering the royalty required worthy of a trial ; for if it could be proved that a similarly constructed velocipede had been introduced into the country before the date of application, the inventor being an alien, the patent would be void; or it would be rendered null also, if the patentee had neglected to put into market and continue the sale of the invention, within eighteen months after the date of patent. Others still, including most of the carriage-makers and machinists of note in the country, who had gone into this business, took pains to have legal advice upon the subject. A meeting was finally held by them ; and the result was a determination to purchase State and city rights, for the use of his patent, of Mr. Witty.

We give the names of the prominent firms and parties who have received licenses for the manufacture and sale of velocipedes, under Patent No. 59,915 : —

Wm. P. Sargent & Co., and John P. Whittier, Boston, Mass., Massachusetts, Vermont, and New Hampshire, excepting the cities of New Bedford, Taunton, Fall River, and Fair Haven, Mass. ; Kimball Bros.,

Boston, for the State of Maine; Wood Bros., Connecticut, excepting one shop right; Pickering & Davis, New York City, one shop right; Mercer & Monod, New York City, one shop right; C. Merrill and Sons, Brooklyn, one shop right. G. L. Brownell, New Bedford, Mass., New Bedford exclusive; G. C. Elliott, Providence, R. I., Rhode Island exclusive. J. M. Quimby, Newark, N. J., New Jersey exclusive.

Mr. Witty now has his hands full of business; employs three clerks to write for him constantly, and has fallen upon a mine of wealth, if he succeeds in maintaining the validity of his claim. He charges the manufacturers ten dollars apiece, royalty, for every machine turned out. If a maker, however, obtains a license to manufacture less than a hundred, he pays fifteen dollars royalty; if under twenty, twenty-five dollars apiece.

Sargent and Whittier, of Boston, and many others of the manufacturers, who have purchased State and town rights, have sent out within their limits circulars similar to those of Mr. Witty, but with the following N. B. attached : —

" Those using the two-wheeled velocipedes, not manufactured under a license, and not having the proper stamp, are also liable for infringement upon said letter patent."

We present an engraving taken from the Patent Office Reports, showing the Lallement patent of

1866. In this *veloce* the cranks, F, are points of great interest, as the claim is for the combination of these treadle cranks with the two wheels A and B, reach C, guiding arms D, and the fork in which the front wheel is hung. We attribute the unpopularity of the old dandy-horse to its lack of these cranks, while the great success of the modern *veloce* is due to the crank application. In this *veloce* it will be noticed that the reach, C, extends over the rear wheel, and a V brace on each side of the wheel connects the axle to the reach. With this style of reach or frame, it was found very difficult to construct a *veloce* sufficiently steady to run with any degree of satisfaction.

There is still another New York patentee, Stephen W. Smith, who claims that the so-called French Velocipede is an American invention, perfected in this country, and introduced into France by patent, and personally by himself; and that the idea was stolen from him by the French manufacturers. He obtained his patent in 1862, for a " cantering propeller " for children, or hobby-horse mounted on wheels ; and considers his patent to include the combinations used upon all velocipedes, and threatens to prosecute infringements;

This patent has lately been reissued for the purpose of widening the claims and to attempt to cover the whole ground occupied by the patent bicycle of M. Lallement. The reissued claim is as follows :—

" 1st claim, in combination with a saddle-seat for the rider, the employment and use of a cranked axle, arms, and foot-rest, so arranged that the power applied by the feet of the rider shall give motion to the vehicle, substantially as described and specified.

" 2. The combination of the following elements, namely, a saddle-seat for the rider, a cranked axle, for propelling the vehicle by power applied by the feet of the rider, and a steering mechanism so constructed that the direction of travel of the vehicle may be governed by the rider, substantially as described and specified.

" 3. The universal joint, in combination with the fulcrum of the vehicle, and the steering wheel, constructed and operating substantially as, and for, the purposes specified.

" 4. The hinged legs in combination with the body of the horse, and with the cranks substantially as and for the purposes specified.

" 5. The foot-rests upon the arms, substantially as and for the purposes specified.

" 6. The double-armed levers, and diagonal cords, in combination with the handle and steering wheel, substantially as described and specified."

The first and second claims are intended to embrace, and do embrace, as far as words can accomplish it, the essential elements of the velocipede now in use. It remains to be determined by the courts how far the rival claimants clash with each other. The manufacturers have as yet paid but very little attention to the demands of Mr. Smith.

In 1867, the Hanlon Brothers devised an improved style of reach, consisting of a bifurcated bar, or fork, in the jaws of which the hind wheel is allowed to revolve ; while the single end of this fork forms part of the swivel, over the front wheel. Not yet satisfied with this *veloce*, on account of the difficulty they found in using the same machine for their in-door performances, and out-door exhibitions, they had the saddle arranged so as to be enabled to vary its position nearer to, or farther from, the front wheel, and at the same time had slots made in the cranks, so that the treadle might be adjusted to various lengths. The alterations were found to be of such benefit, that application for a patent covering these improvements was made by them, and granted by the Patent Office. We know of no velocipedes now being made in this country, which do not include in their construction all these late improvements, and the Hanlons are also notifying manufacturers of the existence of their claims.

The Patent powers in Washington are literally

overwhelmed with applications for patents of different models of these articles. In a large room in the Patent Office, there are some four hundred of these models awaiting investigation. Over eighty models have already been examined and patents for them issued; others are now under examination. Some hundred caveats or notices that patents will be applied for have been lately filed. In one week eighty applications and caveats were received. One single agency in New York city has lately prepared seventy patents for improvements.

THERE is a very general complaint of the high prices maintained by the manufacturers of velocipedes, and it is claimed that they are pocketing immense receipts, at the expense of an excited and incautious public. Though there is no doubt that they can be manufactured at prices much below those at which the best machines are now held, and still yield a handsome profit, a reduction in price will not be probable so long as the demand so far exceeds the supply. And now that it is found that the machine is patented, we will not have the so much wished for cheap velocipede, which would assuredly have followed the competition that had commenced, before it was known that one man only held the exclusive right to their manufacture.

But it must be remembered that as long as materials and labor are so dear, the cost of manufacture must necessarily be great. A manufacturer requires draughtsmen to design his improvements, pattern-makers to prepare models for the foundry, blacksmiths to do the forging, wheelwrights for the

wheels, machinists to turn and fit the work, foundry-
men to cast the pedals and braces, bolt-makers to
make the rivets and bolts, saddlers to prepare the
seats, and painters and varnishers to finish the
machine for the wareroom. The wear and tear in
the ordinary use of the velocipede is so great as to
require the very best of material in its construction.
There is no other kind of vehicle which receives
such severe usage. The weight of the rider and the
concussions of the road are not only borne by two
wheels, but the necessity of giving the fore wheel
a sidewise motion, render it indispensable to connect the two by a frame, whose peculiar form and
character make it exceedingly liable to be deranged
and broken. This frame and its appendages must
be of wrought iron, steel, and brass, and all its work
must be of the best quality, or else the machine will
soon get out of order and become useless. The fit-
tings of the two wheels, their axles and their journals, must also be of the best workmanship. The
same is true of the wheels themselves. No wood
that is not perfectly seasoned should be used for
them; and the hubs, spokes, and felloes must be
built with the utmost care and thoroughness; otherwise they will soon become wabbling and unsteady,
so that speed and comfort will be out of the ques-
tion.

The price of a good machine will not fall much

below a hundred dollars, until there is a general decline in the price of all sorts of commodities.

We advise the purchaser, by all means, to get a *good machine*. It is now possible to buy cheap velocipedes; and they will, no doubt, be manufactured much cheaper, and yet be dear at any price. The best are none too good, and are certainly worth more than the difference.

The hall velocipedes are, for the most part, slim affairs; the frame made entirely of cast iron, without metal gearings, brakes, or springs, and useful only for floors. It is uncomfortable for the rider to go over roughnesses without springs, and a well-built machine is required to stand the jar of uneven roads.

It is no better policy to purchase a cheap velocipede, than a cheap ready-made shoe or other article of clothing.

It is a prevalent but erroneous idea, that the larger the bicycle, the greater the beauty and the greater the speed. A machine with a front wheel of a diameter of forty inches, is the largest that can possibly be rendered practicable. Thirty-eight inches is much better; and good riders prefer that of but thirty-six or thirty-seven inches diameter for the road.

Before purchasing any machine, especially the cheaper ones, examine them thoroughly; or if not a judge of good mechanical workmanship, ask a friend to do it for you. Many defects are concealed by the coatings of paint, particularly in the castings and forgings; and a machine that is weak in any point, is a dangerous one in fast riding. Be sure that every bolt is properly secured by nuts that cannot be shaken off; they should be riveted into the bolt, as they will soon work loose if not so fastened, The crank should never be keyed into the shaft, but fastened on to a square head; or, what is better, shrunk into the shaft.

The ingenious way of supporting lanterns on the machine, is a waste of time and expense; better some kind of clamps to secure a light umbrella in front, when the sun shines hot, or it rains; and clamps for fastening a travelling bag or shawl in the rear, particularly if one looks forward to country excursions and summer trips.

To those who have never seen the two-wheeled velocipede in use, it seems surprising that the rider can keep his equilibrium. The principle of the thing is the same as that of the movement of a boy's hoop. As long as the hoop revolves rapidly, its tendency to any lateral movement is almost suspended, and the greater the speed the less the difficulty in maintaining the upright position.

At first sight one supposes it to be a formidable undertaking to mount and steer the bicycle. To learn to manage it, however, requires no more skill, courage, or patience, than to learn the art of skating; and when the art is once acquired, it provides a means of locomotion and a source of enjoyment as much more available than skating, as the number of days in the year is greater than the few bright mornings when one can find a smooth, glassy, and well-frozen skating ground.

" Velocipedestrianism " is fully the equal of skating and horseback riding, in its invigorating and exhilarating effects. The velocipede bears young and old, light and heavy, easily and pleasantly and with equal facility.

In learning the velocipede, it is advisable to use a machine of only moderate height, so that the soles of the feet can readily touch the ground. At the best school we know, where the pupils graduate experts, six different sizes of machines are used. The beginner is put upon one with a guiding wheel of a diameter of only thirty-four inches, and is promoted from one to another, according to progress.

At first start, run beside the iron horse, leading it by the hand, so as to familiarize yourself with its movements, and to master well in you mind the idea of the fore wheel, upon which all depends. This will be an affair of but a few moments only. You will very readily perceive that it will be impossible to balance upon the machine, while it is standing still. You will also see that, without practice, it will be an impossibility to mount the iron horse, and balance yourself upon the seat, while it is in motion. Both these facts lead you to perceive that motion is the first requisite. To get that, and at the same time maintain equilibrium, you must first use your feet on the floor or ground as a means of progression, learning, as you move, to balance yourself by the motion of the guide wheel, to the right or left, whichever way you may lean.

If out-of-doors, it is as well to practice on a slope;

and after mounting, let the machine move forward of its own accord, while you occupy yourself studying the effect produced by the inclination which you give to the balancing pole or handle. After you .have practiced enough to admit of your going some little way without touching your feet, learn to go the same distance with your legs raised, so as to bring the centre of gravity higher from the base. When you have overcome this difficulty and thoroughly understand the action of the balancing pole, place one foot on the pedal, and follow its movements, without assisting them. Then try the other foot, and accustom yourself to the movement of turning the wheels with your feet. Next, put both feet upon the pedals, and work them alternately with scrupulous regularity. Speed is attained by simply accelerating this movement. You will be surprised to find that you can, all at once, ride your velocipede. After a couple of hours of proper practice, you will be able to accomplish a distance of thirty or forty vards, without running the risk of an upset.

In learning, be careful to keep the shoulders straight and the head back. An erect position upon the bicycle is as necessary for grace and ease, as upon the horse. Avoid looking at the wheels, but accustom yourself to look ahead.

Confidence in your own ability is required, without rashness. If you practice in a public hall, pay no attention to the laughter of spectators, and avoid self-consciousness. If you feel that no one was ever so clumsy before, the feeling itself will be sure to increase your awkwardness. Remember that all good riders have necessarily been through the same experience. It is no disgrace to upset your vehicle. Molière says : " *On peut être honnête homme et faire mal des vers.*"

Take things as easy as possible. The greatest difficulty with beginners is to restrain the unnecessary expenditure of muscular power. They ordinarily perform ten times the amount of labor requisite. They use all the force they can, in pressing upon the pedals, and clasp the handle in front, as if hanging on for dear life. Do not strain the muscles of the arms. There is no necessity for it, or for any violent muscular effort. A good rider can obtain the greatest speed upon the road with half the exertion used by the novice in learning the first movements.

If the day after your first attempt you feel a little lame and sore, remember that it is nothing more than you would feel after riding horseback for the first time, or after taking gentle but unaccustomed exercise in a gymnasium.

If you finish your first trial covered with dust and perspiration, with a bumped head, jammed feet, tired arms, and sore muscles, let your faith remain triumphant, and your determination and expectation to master the vehicle increased.

But with proper caution there is no danger either of falls or hurt in using the velocipede in the way we have advised. The pedal is constructed so that the foot of the rider can at once leave it; and should the machine incline to one side, it is only necessary to remove the foot from the same side, and place it on the ground. One must not let the handles go; they seem to restore and maintain the balance of the machine after the rider is off it. In alighting, both feet should be raised from the pedal at the same instant, which slackens the speed of the machine, and placed upon the ground simultaneously.

If you learn in a school or rink, you will find a rough pine floor much the best for practice. Floors that are sprinkled with sawdust, or sanded, are apt to cause the machine to slip in turning.

In your first practice, avoid trying experiments, or doing too much; but watch your position in the saddle, and perfect yourself in the balance movement. After that is perfectly learned, try to ride slowly, and practice with your feet upon the rest in front. It will of course require much experience before you are able to dash along the paved streets or country roads, or to try the tricks and fancy movements of an expert. Perseverance, however, makes perfect; and if you persist, you will be able, in due time, to ride side-saddle fashion, to pick up your hat from the floor, to take off your coat while going at full speed, and even to stand upon the saddle.

Some learn to ride in three hours, some in three days, and occasionally we hear of a timid and stupid scholar, for whom three months will scarcely suffice. It depends upon the machine, the method of going to work, and the quickness and adaptability of the rider. The knowledge often comes suddenly. We have seen those who have tried to learn for days without success, suddenly mount their veloces and start around a hall, astonished at the ease with which they maintained their balance, and looking as pleased as if they had accomplished the object of their existence. A few hours' practice usually makes a student quite the master of ceremonies.

As soon as you have acquired the knowledge, you will wonder how amateurs can be so awkward, and be surprised that you found it so difficult.

Should the velocipede upon which you learn be too high to practice in the way we have indicated, you should have some one hold the machine for the first trial, the hands upon the back extremity of the bar upon which you sit, so as to in no way impede the action of the fore wheel.

To those who wish to learn, we would especially suggest the spring, fall, and winter months. It is too warm to learn in summer, that being the season to reap the reward of early exertion. Velocipede riding is the easiest thing imaginable when one knows how to ride properly.

CONSTRUCTION OF THE BICYCLE.

THE accompanying engraving will convey to the mind of the reader a correct idea of the French two-wheeled velocipede. The majority of makers in this country fashion their machine upon this pattern in every essential respect. We append a full technical description.

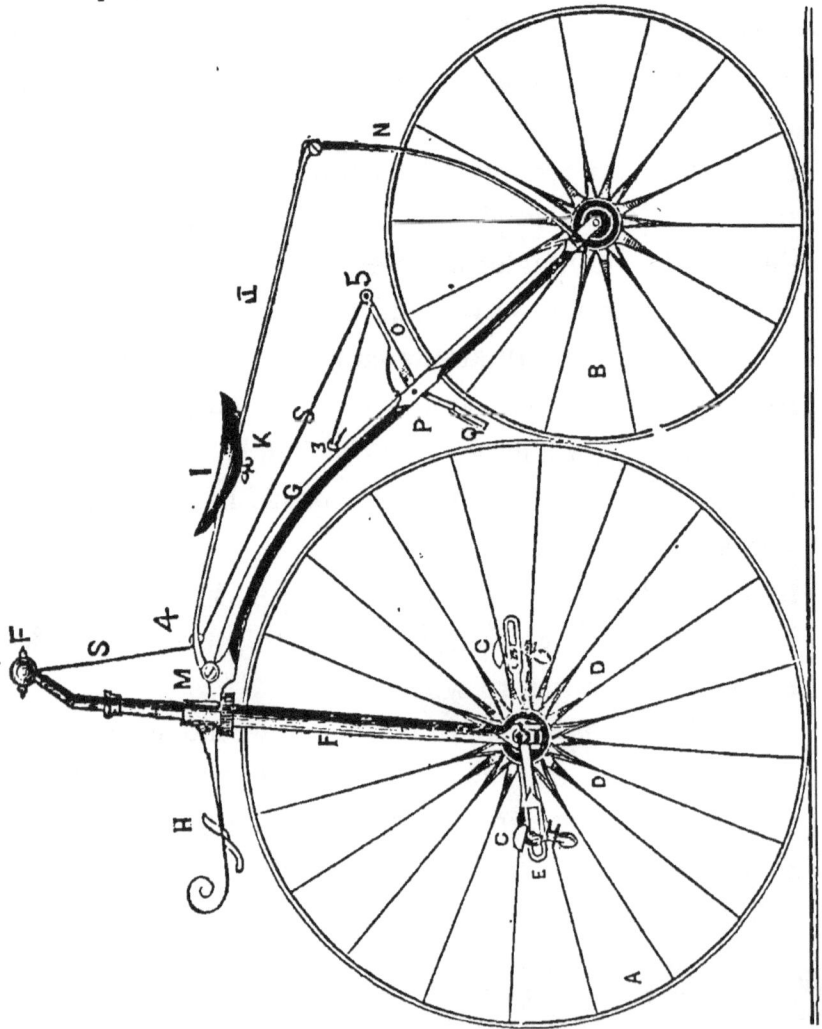

A is the front wheel. This is the steering wheel, and upon its axis the power is applied. B is the hind wheel; C, the treadles or foot-pieces; D, the treadle cranks; E, slots in cranks, by which to adjust the foot-pieces and accommodate the length to the legs of the rider; F, bifurcated jaw, the lower part of which forms the bearing for the axle of the front wheel. From the upper part of this jaw a rod or pivot extends, to which is attached the steering arm or handle F; G, the reach or perch, extending from the jaw of the front wheel to the rear or hind wheel. This reach is bifurcated, forming jaws for the hind wheel. H, "rests" on the front part of the reach. The rider puts one leg on the rest and works one of the cranks with the other leg while riding "side-saddle," or a leg may be placed upon each rest when the velocipede has acquired sufficient momentum, and the rider does not wish to keep his feet upon the treadles. I, the saddle or seat, which is adjustable on the seat-spring L, by the thumb-screw K. The seat-spring L, is attached at M to the reach G, which, at the other end, is fastened to the spring-struts N, that rise from the reach G; O, the brake-lever, on the fulcrum P; Q, the "shoe" of the brake that acts against the periphery of the hind wheel. The brake is operated by means of the cord S, one end of which is attached to the steering handle F, and the other end to the reach at 3. A cord passes from the steering handle under the pulley or roller 4, thence over the pulley 5, on the brake-lever O, and from there to the point 3, where it is attached to the reach G. The brake is operated by giving a slight turning motion to the handle F, thus winding a small sheave upon the axis of the handle, and bringing the shoe Q, of the brake-lever O, in contact with the surface of the wheel B.

VARIETIES OF THE BICYCLE.

THE best two-wheeled velocipedes manufactured in this country, are those of Messrs. Pickering & Davis, Wood Brothers, Mercer & Monod, and Calvin Witty, New York City; and William P. Sargent & Co., and Kimball Brothers, Boston, Mass.

WOOD BROTHERS' VELOCIPEDE.

The Wood Brothers, of 596 Broadway, New York, decided at the commencement of the *furore* in this country, to make the manufacture of velocipedes an important branch of their business. They made thorough and personal investigation of the many styles used abroad, and selected the patents of

Messrs. Michaux & Co., as being the one most in favor with experts there.

The Wood Brothers' velocipede, though very similar to the French machine, is made of better material, with steel tires and axles, and with gun-metal gearings upon the rear wheel. This machine combines in a great degree lightness and durability. It weighs from fifty to fifty-eight pounds, and if required, can easily be led, lifted, or even carried by the rider. The seat is fixed more directly over the stirrups than in some machines, and at such a height above the wheels as to avoid wear and tear of the clothing from contact with mud and dirt, and the driving wheel in turning. The stirrups are attached in such a manner to the crank, that they can be adjusted near the hub or axle, giving speed on level roads; or they can be placed at the end of the crank, giving power and ease for rough roads and ascending grades. Two kinds of stirrups are used; the " spool pattern," entirely round, and covered with leather, making it easy for the beginner to keep his foot in place; and the French swing stirrup, which is for proficient riders and general use. This latter style has a very long bearing, relieving the strain on the ankle joint, and making it easy to ride a distance without fatigue.

This bicycle has a brake, rests for the feet in front, and a handsomely finished saddle, supported by steel springs. It will ascend a grade of one foot in twenty. The price is $135.

The Wood Brothers have in their possession the first velocipede ever brought into this country. When first exhibited on the sidewalk in front of their warerooms, it attracted such attention that the police requested them to remove it. They have just completed for a New York gentleman, at a price of $300, one of the most completely finished veloci-pedes yet manufactured in America.

THE MONOD VELOCIPEDE.

Messrs. Mercer & Monod, of 54 William Street, New York, manufacture their velocipedes after a model of their own, which has its advantages, and embraces many of the best points of the French machine.

The steering post is inclined backward, which brings the handle within easy reach of the body, and the whole machine under perfect control; and gives it a particularly rakish and natty appearance upon the road. The saddle can be adjusted backward or forward, according to the length of limb of the rider.

Messrs. Mercer & Monod use the triangular beveled treadle and an improved brake. The defect of this machine is its weight, which is about seventy pounds. Some riders, however, prefer a heavier machine than others, and recommend the Monod velocipede on this account.

A good rider on this machine can obtain a speed of ten or twelve miles an hour. It varies in price from $110 to $150, according to finish.

These gentlemen have lately manufactured some very complete machines for country use, with shawl rack, mud dasher, etc.

WITTY'S VELOCIPEDE.

Calvin Witty, of 638 Broadway, New York, models his velocipedes almost entirely after those of Messrs. Michaux & Co. When he commenced their manufacture, he tried by various experiments to improve upon the original patent. Most of his attempts proved unsuccessful. Among other proposed improvements, he endeavored to apply the brake to the front wheel, but found that it would stop the machine on the instant, and throw the rider headlong; and that such a brake, though suitable for a steam-engine, could not be rendered practicable upon a velocipede.

These machines are made of wrought iron, with brakes, springs, improved saddle, and gun-metal bearings. As Mr. Witty has the exclusive right of

M. Lallement's patent upon the two-wheeled velocipede, he can afford to manufacture at a somewhat
cheaper rate than those who are obliged to pay a
royalty. His bicycles range in price from $90 to $130.

Mr. Witty's first machines were not so good as
some of other manufacturers, but he has lately improved upon them. They are a little heavier than
those of Messrs. Sargent & Co., Pickering & Davis,
and Wood Brothers, but equal to any in durability
and finish.

Mr. Witty is at present constructing a velocipede
which he anticipates will run a mile in one minute
and twenty seconds, or faster than any trotting-horse
can ever be expected to go ; the driving wheel is to
be so constructed that it will revolve three times
while the treadles are once making their circuit.

PICKERING'S AMERICAN VELOCIPEDE.

As will be seen from the accompanying engraving,
" Pickering's American Velocipede," manufactured
by Messrs. Pickering & Davis, 144 Greene Street,
New York, differs very materially from the French
model, so generally used by other manufacturers. It
is claimed that it is more simple and durable, lighter
and stronger.

The reach or frame of this velocipede is made of hydraulic tubing. The gun-metal bearings are so attached that, when worn, they may be replaced by others, which are interchangeable like the parts of sewing-machines and fire-arms. The axle is so constructed as to constitute, in itself, an oil box. It is made tubular, and closed at either end with a screw, on the removal of which it is filled with lard oil.

Cotton lamp-wick is placed loosely in the tubular axle and the oil is by this means fed to the bearing, as fast as required, through the small holes made for the purpose in the centre of the axle. The saddle is supported on a spiral spring, giving an elastic seat; it is brought well back, so that the rider maintains an erect position, and is adjustable to suit the length of limb of the rider. The tiller or steering handle is constructed with a spring, so that the hands are relieved from the jolting that they would otherwise receive while running over rough ground. The stirrups or crank pedals, are three-sided, with circular flanges at each end, fitted to turn on the crank pins, so that the pressure of the foot will always bring one of the three sides into proper position. They are so shaped as to allow of the use of the fore part of the foot, bringing the ankle joint into play, relieving the knee, and rendering propulsion easier than when the shank of the foot alone is used. The connecting apparatus differs from that of the French vehicle in that the saddle bar serves only as a seat and brake, and is not attached to the rear wheel. By a simple pressure forward against the tiller, and a backward pressure against the tail of the saddle, the saddle spring is compressed, and the brake attached to it brought firmly down against the wheel.

Messrs. Pickering & Davis have a large manufactory, and are the constant recipients of orders from all parts of the country. Mr. Pickering has always been a practical machinist, and personally superintends the structure of each machine turned out.

A rider upon the Pickering velocipede can average ten or twelve miles an hour. On good roads they have been ridden, for short distances, at the rate of eighteen miles an hour. It is claimed that they will easily ascend a grade of from one foot in twenty to one in fifteen.

The price varies from $110 to $155. A very complete, finely finished one, can be bought for $150. This is an expensive machine; but many *connoisseurs* think its advantages over other bicycles fully merit the small difference in price. Many experts use it altogether for fancy riding, and many who have tried all kinds upon the road, think this much to be preferred.

SARGENT VELOCIPEDE.

Wm. P. Sargent & Co., of 155 Tremont Street, Boston, have many excellent facilities, in connection with their extensive works for the construction of pleasure carriages, for the manufacture of velocipedes. They foresaw the *furore* that would arise in this country before its commencement, and made early preparations to engage largely in the manufacture of the Parisian novelty.

Their machines are made upon the French plan, with all the American improvements, in form, material, and thoroughness of construction. They are very similar to those made by the Wood Brothers, but have important merits of their own. The hind wheel turns on the axle bar, preventing the friction upon the bearing, as in other machines in which the axle turns with the wheel. The neck of the machine is wrought in one piece, and the head of the swivel in the neck is of wrought iron, square in shape. The fork of the steering bar is of wrought iron also, instead of the cast brass usually used. This makes a delicate part of the machine very durable, for it is a rule in mechanics that one metal will act upon itself with less friction than upon another kind of metal. The best workmen are employed and the best material used. The tires and axles are of the finest steel, and the bearings of the finest gun-metal. The saddle is adjustable and can be readily moved backward or forward.

Messrs. Sargent & Co. use both the three-sided beveled and the swing treadle, either of which always present a surface to the foot, so that after mounting or removing the foot temporarily, no time is lost in replacing it.

They have made every effort to construct a light, noiseless, steady-running, completely-finished, and perfect machine. Their price is from $110 to $150.

Messrs. Sargent & Co. also manufacture a cheaper machine, without springs, much like those manufactured by Mr. Brownell of New Bedford. This machine is sold for $55, and is used with satisfaction in halls and rinks.

Mr. Sargent has on hand in his warerooms a large

assortment of machines of other manufacturers, including those of Wood Brothers, Mercer & Monod, and Pickering & Davis.

. ———————

KIMBALL'S VELOCIPEDE.

Messrs. Kimball Brothers & Co., of 110, 112, and 114 Sudbury Street, Boston, secured the first license granted in this country under the Lallement patent, giving them the exclusive right to manufacture in Maine, and the liberty of selling throughout the United States. They have long enjoyed a high reputation for elegant sleighs and carriages, and at their commencement of the manufacture of velocipedes, determined to maintain their reputation in this new and important branch of their business. Their velocipedes are also patterned from those of Messrs. Michaux & Co., with such improvements as are in use with the best manufacturers.

The frames of these machines are of wrought iron and steel, with composition and gun-metal bearings, steel levers, and axles, and superior saddles. Even into the lowest priced machines, they put the best stock in every part. Messrs. Kimball Brothers' velocipedes vary in price from $75 to $175, according to style and finish. The most expensive are furnished with mud fenders, lamps, and silver-plated brakes. A very fine one can be obtained for $135. Their cheaper bicycles are, without doubt, as good as any in the market. They are light, durable, built of wrought-iron, and *furnished with springs.*

The New England manufacturers of two-wheeled velocipedes, next in prominence to Messrs. Sargent & Kimball, are William H. Brownell & Co., of New Bedford, George E. Elliott, of Providence, and Messrs. Dalzell & Sons, of South Egremont.

William H. Brownell & Co., of New Bedford, manufacture only the cheaper kind of velocipedes. The frame or reach, which curves over the rear wheel, is built of wrought iron. The machine is without springs or metal gearings. This is used almost exclusively in the New England schools and rinks; and for the use of the beginner, or on smooth floors, gives merited satisfaction. It is not as suitable for the road, or as easy for the rider, as the more expensive machines, which are furnished with springs, brakes, and rests for the feet. But for those who wish to have a bicycle, with as small an expenditure as possible, this machine will answer as well as any that we know. It is firm and durable, moderately light, and does not get easily out of repair.

Messrs. Brownell & Co. have sold $40,000 worth

of machines in the last three months, and the demand is far greater than the supply. They are as heavily engaged in the business as any manufacturers in the country. The price varies from $70 to $90. A good machine of Mr. Brownell's make can be obtained for $75.

George C. Elliott, of Providence, has purchased a license under the Lallement patent, for the exclusive manufacture of the two-wheeled velocipede in Rhode Island. He combines the French machine with the usual American improvements. The prices are the same as are demanded for other good machines.

Those who have used Mr. Elliott's bicycles claim that they are the equal of any manufactured.

Messrs. Dalzell & Sons, of South Egremont, Massachusetts, manufacture a velocipede which has many of the merits of that of the Wood Brothers. Their velocipede works are at Hudson, N. Y., and there is a steadily increasing demand for their machines. The prices vary from $125 to $150.

G. F. Perkins & Co., of Haydenville, Mass., advertise to furnish a velocipede with steel springs for $40. We do not know that their machine has been fairly tested. We have never seen it in use, and are unable to speak of its merits.

Among the latest improved machines, is one manufactured by Messrs. Tomlinson, Demarest, & Co., No. 620 Broadway, New York. It is called the "Improved American Velocipede," and differs from styles best known to the public in important respects. It is the recipient of many encomiums from those who have learned to ride it.

The iron arms, between which the front wheel is held, are inclined back at an angle of forty-five degrees from the perpendicular, which inclination brings the seat in such a relative position to the forewheel, that a man of medium height can, with his feet, reach the treadles of one of these velocipedes, the front wheel of which is forty-five inches in diameter, with as much ease as he can those of the ordinary velocipede, the fore wheel of which is of a diameter seven or eight inches smaller. This peculiarity gives likewise great facility in describing sharp curves and circles of small diameter, the body being inclined in the direction in which the rider wishes to propel himself, and in the direction in which the driving wheel is inclined. Those who have become expert in the use of this new machine, claim that the movement of the body in propelling and guiding it, is more nearly analogous to that of skating, than is employed in controlling the ordinary bicycle. Indeed, they claim that it can be guided by the mere inclination of the body without perceptibly varying the pressure upon the handles to the one side or the other.

The peculiar rakish arrangement of the standard, prevents the usual jar to the guiding arms in going over rough ground and pavements, and allows the wheel to turn without soiling the pantaloons. It is claimed that this machine can be driven at great speed, and up steep grades.

Messrs. Pearsall Brothers, of New York, have patented a bicycle which is so constructed that the rear wheel is used as a guiding wheel. This machine will turn a quick corner, and can be ridden rapidly. Its price is $125.

Stephen W. Smith, of 90 William Street, New York, manufactures a velocipede for boys, with a guiding wheel twenty inches in diameter, for $25. The saddle of this machine is so wide that but little balancing power is requisite, and any child can easily learn to ride it.

THE DEXTER BICYCLE.

The Dexter bicycle only differs from other two-wheeled machines in one respect. This, however, is quite important. By a simple and effective device, it admits of an instantaneous connection and disconnection of the crank with the axle of the driving wheel, keeping the treadles stationary or in motion, at the will of the rider, while the wheel continues to revolve. . Ordinarily, in obtaining a high rate of speed on a velocipede, the rapidity of the revolution of the crank becomes too great to be followed by the movement of the feet, except at the expenditure of too much exertion. This difficulty is wholly obviated by Mr. Dexter. A continuous and uniform rate of speed may be kept up with his machine without fatiguing the rider.

THE CHICAGO VELOCIPEDE.

This velocipede is manufactured by Messrs. Loring & Keene, of Chicago, Illinois, and has become very popular in that city and throughout the West. It is a light machine, somewhat similar to that of Pickering & Davis. The saddle is upon a spiral spring, is not connected with the rear wheel, and serves as a seat and brake. The manufacturers claim that it will ascend a grade of one foot in eighteen, and that it can be driven at great speed. Its price is $130.

D. W. Gosling, of Cincinnati, Ohio, has been engaged for some months in the manufacture of a velocipede upon the Franco-American plan. He claims that his bicycle is equal to any other, both in durability and fine workmanship.

There is another manufactory in Cincinnati, which turns out sixteen hundred velocipedes per week, that are sold at $35 each. These machines are of the poorest possible workmanship and material.

There are large numbers of bicycles in the market which are both unsafe and dangerous, and which the makers push into unsuspecting hands by offering them at much reduced rates. Many portions of these which should be of wrought iron, are made of cast iron, of course attractively painted. Nothing should be cast about the metal works of a velocipede except the brasses.

A bad machine carefully kept, may, perhaps, last longer than a good machine very badly managed. It should be the ambition of a good rider, however, to have a good machine, kept in good order. There is danger to the velocipedist in pushing ahead with speed, when the slightest collision, or the giving way of some minute portion of the machine, may smash the whole affair.

FOUR-WHEELED VELOCIPEDES.

BRADFORD'S VELOCIPEDE.

IF any of our readers desire the luxury of a ride on a velocipede without the necessity of taking lessons, or the danger of getting a fall, they will find " Bradford's Four-Wheeled Velocipede " ready and able to afford them the pleasure.

The inventor of this vehicle, Mr. C. K. Bradford, has devoted the greater part of the last five years to experiments upon the velocipede, and took out his first patent three years and a half ago. The machine, as now constructed and improved, obtained its American patent October 13th, 1868. It has since been patented in England, France, and Belgium. It is made of the best material, and finished like a gentleman's trotting wagon. It weighs but sixty-five pounds, and combines in a high degree both lightness and strength. Any man, woman or child, can learn to guide it easily with but a few moments practice.

The inventor claims that it is able to maintain a speed of a mile in three minutes, and that the extraordinary time of a half mile in one minute and forty-five seconds, has been made upon a country road. It can be driven by almost any man, at the rate of a mile in four minutes, on almost any road, without greater exertion than is ordinarily used in walking. This velocipede, unlike all others, is seen to best advantage on the street. In Mr. Bradford's tasteful little curricle, the rider can sit at ease as carelessly as in a carriage, giving himself up wholly to the exhilaration of the rapid movement, and the pleasurable exercise of the muscles, which is just enough to make the machine skim over the ground, and give an enjoyable sense of power. The increase of friction, which would naturally result from the additional number of wheels, is prevented by an application of anti-friction rollers, which reduce the labor of propelling the machine to a minimum, a requisite of the highest importance to a person seeking either recreation or utility.

This velocipede has an adjustable seat, which may be placed nearer or further from the pedal crank, to suit the rider's length of limb. The seat is furnished with a high, strong back, which, besides adding materially to the rider's comfort, serves him as a *point d'appui*, a firm base from which he can exert a powerful force in propelling.

The steering device is simple and complete, and is the same principle upon which one guides the horse. It is guided by the hands, and the large rear wheels are operated upon by means of a wheel and cord arrangement, conveniently placed beside the seat. It is claimed that the machine can be steered almost to a hair's breadth. It is used by many city firms for the purpose of carrying messages and parcels, and can be seen upon Broadway in the thickest part of the travel. It does not hesitate at curb-stones, and will run over most roads as easily as any light wagon: It can be ridden up almost any hill without a fatiguing expenditure of force. It offers excellent advantages for carrying refreshments and various articles of light baggage, necessary in a flying trip or excursion.

Though this machine requires more room for its accommodation than the bicycle, and cannot be stored against any wall; and though it does not give the peculiar and fascinating kind of exhilaration which balancing upon the bicycle affords, it will be seen to have many advantages over the two-wheeled vehicle.

This velocipede is especially adapted to ladies, and

allows the rider to sit as becomingly and gracefully as she would in her carriage or her parlor chair. The proprietors have a very ingenious device which can be attached to the machine for ladies, which completely conceals all points of motion.

The Bradford Brothers have a large manufactory in Newark, N. J. Mr. J. W. Thorp is their agent, and is rapidly selling State and county rights. This velocipede is sold at $150.

The Messrs. Bradford also manufacture a smaller size for boys, complete in every particular, for $75.

CALLAHAN'S VELOCIPEDE.

This velocipede was patented January 5th, 1869, and is on exhibition at 17 State Street, Boston. It has been thoroughly tested and is pronounced a complete success. It will be seen that it is very different from Bradford's machine. The front wheels are used as guiding wheels, the rear as the driving ones. It is propelled by both hands and feet, acting together or separately. The propelling power is almost unlimited, and is furnished by cranks in the hind axles, with lever attachments. It has three different steering arrangements, either of which can be applied, according to the taste of the purchaser.

In all these, the forward wheel and axle are turned with a lever arrangement, operated upon by the hand.

The machine develops both chest and limbs, and can be readily used by ladies and children. A little girl of six years has ridden it for an hour without fatigue. It is so constructed, that scruples of delicacy need prevent no lady from driving it. It can be driven either backwards or forwards, will run upon the road, at the rate of fifteen miles an hour, and will ascend any ordinary hill with ease. It is claimed, that it is the only machine made that can be checked in going down hill, or that can be stopped instantly.

The machine varies in size and weight. That most in favor, has a wheel of three feet and a half in diameter, and a weight of about one hundred pounds. It is constructed of the best material, and is neat and nobby in appearance. Its price is $125.

THE TRICYCLE.

THE generic tricycle, or three-wheeled velocipede, as used abroad, is not likely to meet with general favor in this country.

In its steering arrangements and mode of propulsion, its construction is similar to that of the bicycle. The rear wheels are large and light; the fore wheel is smaller, and serves to guide the machine, being acted upon by means of the steering bar or handle, which causes it to bend in the direction indicated by the rider. The pedals are attached to the front wheel, and are shaped like slippers, which facilitates the movement of the legs, and at the same time admits of the feet being disengaged simultaneously. The movement required to propel this machine is a natural one, does not produce unusual fatigue, and is analogous to that of walking.

The larger three-wheeled velocipedes have a lever which follows the line of the eccentrics attached to the pedals, and fits on to the axles. By assisting the movement of this lever, the speed of the vehicle is considerably increased, and a simple pressure against it checks the rotary motion of the wheel, and stops the progress of the machine. This lever is, in fact, both a means of impulsion and a brake. As this vehicle is chiefly patronized by the fair sex, the seat is more commodious than that of the bicycle; having sides and back of wicker, and a horse-hair cushion.

The tricycle is simply a hack, while the bicycle is a blooded horse that fully demonstrates the "poetry of motion." The tricycle is easier to guide, and safer to ride than the two-wheeled machine; there is however more friction, and its speed is much less rapid. It has, thus far, been found impossible to construct a three-wheeler with the pedal method of propulsion, that could compete with the bicycle in speed or pleasure of driving. Large wheels are necessary for speed. If a guiding wheel be applied to a tricycle of this kind large enough to run rapidly on the road, and to counterbalance the size of the other wheels, it would be unsteady of motion; the rider would be apt to be thrown headlong at any jar, and the whole machine would be rendered unsafe.

Many of the larger manufacturers have built the tricycle to some extent. Most of them have discontinued their make, finding it unprofitable, and that the machine gave but little satisfaction.

The Bradford Brothers of New York City obtained a patent, and entered largely into the business, at considerable expense. They, however, soon stopped the manufacture, and gave exclusive attention to their four-wheeled machines. The three-wheeled velocipedes of Messrs. Kimball Brothers, Boston, seem to be as popular as any in the market; but the sale is mostly local, and but few of them are manufactured.

Various inventors have endeavored to obtain power, by additions to the gearings, in the shape of spring wheels and levers, but with little success. Others have applied the principle of the crank to be turned by the hand, using the hand for steering purposes.

Mr. Wm. H. Hall, of Boston, Mass., has invented a tricycle, which is impelled by a crank, acting upon a small wheel, connected to another by an endless pulley. Every revolution of the crank turns the wheels of the machine once. This machine has not yet been fairly tested.

A mechanic in Indiana also claims to have invented a machine very similar in construction to this of Mr. Hall's.

Messrs. Forbes & Sears of New Bedford, Mass., have invented a machine with two hind wheels running only about five inches apart. It is claimed that the hind wheels are so near together as to run practically as one wheel; and yet the rider can stop the vehicle and maintain his equilibrium.

Messrs. Topliff & Ely of Eleria, Ohio, patented February 23d, 1869, a tricycle, in which, by a simple movement of a lever, the rear wheels can be run into one, and the vehicle instantaneously changed into a bicycle.

A gentleman of Poughkeepsie, N. Y., has invented a machine, in which both the hind wheels are drivers instead of the forward one. They are fastened on independent axles meeting in the centre, connected by a novel arrangement of gearing, so that either wheel can stand as a pivotal point, and the other be driven round it very swiftly. The inventor states that it will turn in less space than any other velocipede.

Mr. John Tremper, of Wilmington, Del., has designed and patented a tricycle in which the front wheel is the driver as usual; but placed so closely to the axle of the hind wheels, as to give almost as complete command over the motions of the machine, in turning corners, as the two-wheeled velocipede.

"The Bennet Velocipede" is characterized by a driving wheel four feet in diameter, and two guiding wheels behind, each about a foot in diameter.

"Samuels' Velocipede" has also a large driving wheel, with small guiding wheels behind. This machine is propelled by hand cranks, connected with corresponding cranks in the driving wheel shaft. The feet are used for steering. The inventor claims that this machine will run twenty-five miles an hour on a level road.

A New Yorker has invented a machine for ladies, which he has placed on exhibition at Pearsall Riding School. The pedals are applied to the rear wheels, and the small wheel in front is guided by a rod, passing back to the hand of the lady occupying the seat.

One or two of the novel tricycles, modeled upon new principles, have proved decided successes.

A gentleman of Ypsilanti, Mich., has invented one that he claims to have ridden from that place to Detroit, a distance of twenty-eight miles, in two hours and forty-eight minutes; and to have made a mile in Ypsilanti in two minutes and thirty seconds. The wheels of this machine are forty-two inches in diameter, and are propelled by means of a double hand-crank, no treadles being used. On each side of the hub of the forward wheel, is a grooved pulley; and attached to the straight portion of the crank are two more pulleys, the four being connected by belts. At each revolution of the pulleys, the vehicle is propelled a distance of sixteen and a half feet; and when an ordinary rate of speed is attained, it runs quite easily. Its weight is forty-nine pounds, and the inventor claims that it will sustain two hundred pounds without danger of collapsing. It can be run on ordinary carriage roads, with comparative ease.

Samuel Marden of Newton Corner, Mass., has lately commenced the manufacture of a three-wheeled velocipede for which he obtained a patent in February, 1868. He calls his machine "a mechanical horse;" it is propelled *by the weight of the rider*, and by friction. It has neither treadles, cranks, or guiding arms. The rider rises in his stirrups as on a trotting horse. The saddle is so arranged that the pressure upon it revolves a gearing wheel, which acts upon a small one connected with the axle of the rear wheel; these wheels are thus made to turn very rapidly. It will be seen that this velocipede is constructed upon an entirely new principle. It is claimed that it can be driven upon the road, at the rate of from ten to fifteen miles an hour. This machine can be used by ladies, with a side-saddle arrangement. Its price is $125. Mr. Marden's velocipede has been tested, and we think he has a fortune in his invention. He has more orders than he can fill, and is prepared to sell State, county, and town rights.

HEMMING'S UNICYCLE, OR "FLYING YANKEE VELOCIPEDE."

———

The single-wheeled velocipede has at length received a palpable body, and "a local habitation and
a name."

Richard C. Hemming of New Haven, Conn., invented the machine herewith represented, two years
ago ; but has only recently brought it into the market
and applied it to practical purposes. The main
wheel has a double rim, or has two concentric rims,
the inner face of the inner one having a projecting
lip for keeping the friction rollers and the friction
driver in place ; each of these being correspondingly
grooved on their peripheries. The frame on which
the rider sits, sustains these friction wheels in double
parallel arms, on the front one of which is mounted
a double pulley, with belts passing to small pulleys
on the axis of the driving wheel. This double wheel
is driven, as seen, by cranks turned by the hands.
The friction of the lower wheel on the surface of
the inner rim of the main wheel, is the immediate
means of propulsion. A small binding wheel, seen

between the rider's legs, serves to keep the bands or belts tight. The steering is effected either by inclining the body to one side or the other, or by the

foot impinging on the ground, the stirrups being hung low for this purpose. By throwing the weight on these stirrups, the binding wheel may be brought more powerfully down on the belts. Over the rider's head is an awning, and there is also a shield in front of his body to keep the clothes from being soiled by mud and wet. When going forward, the driving wheel is kept slightly forward of the centre of gravity by the position of the rider. By this means the power exerted is comparatively small. Every turn of the crank is equivalent to a rotation of the great wheel.

Mr. Hemming says that this machine can be manufactured for fifty dollars, of a weight of only thirty pounds; that it will ascend steep grades, and that it can be driven on the roads with but little exertion, at the rate of twenty or even twenty-five miles an hour. This wheel is of a diameter of from six to eight feet.

Mr. Hemming's boy of thirteen has one five feet in diameter, the first manufactured, crude in construction, and heavier than necessary, which he propels at the rate of a mile in three minutes.

A mechanic of Dubuque, Iowa, has invented a one-wheeled machine, which he calls a velocycle or velocyde. This velocipede is not ridden upon, but transports its rider into the position of "walkist." It is a large wheel or double wheel, made a unit by a light rim of five feet one inch in diameter. The operator steps upon the rim and commences to ascend an endless ladder. It being movable, of course he does not ascend but sets the wheel in motion. The inventor claims that the effort is not greater than the force of muscle required in ordinary locomotion, and that by his arrangement of pulleys, each step gives a complete revolution of the wheel and is equivalent to a stride of eighteen feet. He claims that it will ascend steep grades, will run at the rate of twenty miles an hour, will not weigh over twenty pounds, and that it can be manufactured for $40.

The single wheeled velocipede was perhaps predicted in Ezekiel i. 15–21. A gentleman in Pittsburg, Pa., claims to have invented one, which can be propelled by the combined force of five men, who occupy comfortable seats in the automatic horse. This wheel is ten feet in diameter, and the inventor thinks it can be driven at the rate of twenty miles an hour.

A New York mechanic has devised a monocycle or single machine, which consists of a wheel eight feet in diameter, with a tire six inches wide, or two narrow tires on its outer edges, with two sets of spokes connecting with a double centre, which fills the place of a hub, the two sides of which are two feet and a half apart. The operator is in the middle, and propels the wheel by an apparatus, in which both his weight and his muscles are brought into play.

We present an engraving of an English one-wheeled velocipede. The feet are placed on short stilts, connected with the cranks, one on either side of the rim, while the rider sits upon a steel spring saddle over the whole wheel. The inventor modestly limits the diameter of the wheel to twelve feet, and the number of revolutions to fifty per minute. Twenty-five miles per hour is the speed expected to be reached. The riders of this machine, without the ability to overcome the laws of gravity, would be very likely to get broken bones and noses. It is not likely to come into general use.

———————

Captain Du Boisson, a Frenchman and captain of Prince Napoleon's yacht, "Jerome Napoleon," has invented a velocipede which runs upon water with great facility. It is composed of two parallel tubes of cast iron, cigar-shaped, connected by iron cross-pieces. In the centre is a propelling wheel, covered by a house or drum, on the top of which the person using the vessel sits comfortably in a sort of saddle, with stirrups. By means of these stirrups and a hand crank upon each side, he gives the wheel its motion, precisely as it is given to a velocipede on shore. The novel craft is easily propelled at the rate of six miles an hour.

A gentleman of Poughkeepsie, N. Y., has invented and uses an Ice Velocipede, which he propels with astonishing rapidity. The frame of this velocipede is built like those which are commonly used in this city. It has but one wheel, steered with a bar as in the land machine, but armed with sharp points to prevent its slipping. Instead of the wheel behind are two sharp runners, like those attached to the ice boats.

A Steam Velocipede has also been invented, from
which great speed is expected. The cylinders and
their attachments to the two driving wheels are not
shown. They are placed vertically in front of the
boiler, between it and the seat, and connect with
cranks on the shaft of the driving wheels. The engraving shows the position of the boiler relatively to
the other parts of the machine. The engine is a

direct acting compound engine of two cylinders,
each cylinder two and a half inches diameter, and
five inches stroke. The steering gear consists of an
endless chain over a grooved wheel on the engine
shaft, and passing over a corresponding wheel fixed
between the forked shaft just over the front. The
latter grooved wheel is a wide one, and over it passes
another chain. This latter chain works round the
boss of the front wheel. This arrangement gives

power to the front wheel, so that in turning a corner, this wheel takes a wider sweep than the two driving-wheels, which go first. In travelling on a straight road (backwards) the machine is turned to either side by turning the steering wheel to the opposite side. The boiler is a vertical one, with four tubes, one and a half inches internal diameter, hanging down by the side of the fire-box. The fire-grate is cast with four holes in it to receive the bottom ends of the tubes so as to hold them firmly. Height of boiler, two feet six inches; height of fire-box, fifteen inches; diameter of fire-box, eleven inches; diameter of boiler, fourteen inches. The fire-box and tubes are copper, pressure two hundred pounds; but twenty-five pounds of steam will be equal to a velocipede propelled by the feet.

Philadelphia has recently produced a velocipede of an entirely new style. There are but two wheels, the seat sitting quite low between them. The novelty consists in a cog attached to the guiding-post, by means of which the rear wheel is made to follow directly in the track of the forward wheel. No matter how short the turn, both wheels make it at the same time, and the seat always remains parallel with the driving-wheel. In other machines there is no guide to the rear wheel, and consequently the machine cannot be turned so readily when a collision is threatened. The new machine, which is called the "Keystone," in honor of its native State, is substantially built, and so far as it has been tested in the riding school, is pronounced a success.

There is an ingenious gentleman in Cincinnati, who is at work constructing a velocipede to be propelled by a spring, on the principle of a watch. After winding it up, he calculates that it will move two miles before it will require winding.

A gentleman in Albany has arranged a velocipede to run on railroad tracks. The wheels have flanges to them, so that they cannot leave the rails. The flanges are so arranged as to be removed when occasion requires, so as to make the machine available on ordinary roads. The inventor claims fifty miles an hour.

An expert velocipedestrian in the West, has had rubber tires put upon the wheels of his vehicle; and finds by their use, he can ride in winter over snow and ice without slipping, and that in summer he is much relieved of the jar from roughnesses of roads.

The vast majority of the new velocipedes of which we hear daily, prove total failures on trial. Most of their inventors proceed upon abstract principles, and fall into absurdities, from which previous practical knowledge would have saved them.

VELOCIPEDES FOR LADIES.

———◆———

W𝐸 present a bicycle for ladies, lately invented
and patented by Messrs. Pickering & Davis of New
York City. It will be seen that the reach or frame,
instead of forming a nearly straight line from the
front swivel to the hind axle, follows the curve of the
front wheel until it reaches a line nearly as low as
the hind axle, when it runs horizontally to that point
of the hind wheel. The two wheels being separated
three or four inches, allow of an upright rod being
secured to the reach; around this is a spiral spring,
on which a comfortable, cane-seated, willow-backed
chair is placed. This machine, with a moderate sized
wheel (of thirty to thirty-three inches), will allow
being driven with a great deal of comfort and all the
advantages of the two-wheel veloce. In mounting,

a lady has to step over the reach, at a point only twelve inches from the floor, the height of an ordinary step in a flight of stairs.

A machine for ladies has also been invented by S. T. Derry of Boston, and patented by Messrs. Sargent and Derry, which in construction and appearance is very similar to the one just described. Its saddle is of velvet on springs, giving a perfectly elastic seat; it is furnished with mud fenders in front and behind, and is complete in every respect.

Both these machines have been examined by experts and pronounced satisfactory. It will be readily seen that they obviate many of the difficulties, embarrassments, and objectionable features of the bicycle. They will, doubtless, become popular. While young men have been dashing about on velocipedes, many young women have looked on with envy and emulation. They have not been satisfied with the tricycle designed for their especial use; and have felt it hard that they should be denied the exercise, amusement, risk, dash, and delightful independence, which the bicycle so abundantly affords.

It is possible that our young ladies will rush into velocipeding as they have into skating, and other athletic amusements. It would be a substitute, in many cases, for the expensive luxury of horseback exercise, and has the advantages over it, of convenience and pleasure as well as cost. Velocipeding will be particularly nice for suburban ladies, who have smooth roads around them, over which they may bowl to their hearts' content, and drive themselves from house to house on morning calls. It will not be necessary to keep an ostler, nor to have an attendant to assist in mounting and to accompany the rider. When ready for her ride, a lady may take her horse from the front hall, clean and fresh, mount, and be off. It would be a bright and beautiful day for our land, should a laudable and reasonable ambition once fairly get possession of our young women, to cultivate and develop their physical natures, and to become strong, healthy, robust, and enduring.

A short time since, " The Revolution " published an able article recommending the use of the bicycle to ladies. It has been used by them for some time in a quiet way, and to a much greater extent than is generally supposed. There are classes for ladies in almost every large city; and many are waiting for fine weather, to enjoy the art in the open air, instead of a closely confined room; and to " Witch the world with noble horsemanship."

The idea has been conceived from seeing experts ride side-saddle fashion, and drive the machine with one foot, that ladies might begin by learning the art in that way. This would be well nigh impossible, though it is easy enough after one is proficient. But with a proper teacher of their own sex, and with suitable dresses for preliminary practice, ladies can soon obtain such a command over the vehicle, that they can ride side-saddle wise with perfect ease.

A lady must begin with great moderation, and train her muscles to the work of propulsion, or they will cry out vehemently at first. Above all, she must avoid getting cold, rheumatism, and neuralgia, after being heated by the exercise.

The best school for ladies is established in Boston, and is conducted in a properly private and exclusive manner. It is supplied with a number of lady teachers and assistants, all under the direction of the best " velocipedagogue" in the city. It is in a large hall in a good locality, and is provided with the best French machines, dressing-rooms, and other conveniences. Many good old Boston names are to be found upon the list of pupils. The lessons are twenty-five dollars for a course of instruction, with a guarantee of proficiency.

There is also a school especially designed for ladies, at the corner of Fifth Avenue and Fourteenth Street, New York, at what is known as the Somerville Art Gallery. This has two halls of an area of 3,000 square feet. One of the halls is set apart for beginners, and the other for those more advanced.

Ladies, in riding the bicycle, commonly use the modest and appropriate costume worn by them in calisthenic exercises and in the gymnasium. Another very suitable dress for the *velocipedestrienne* has been thus described : —

" Let the outer dress skirt be made so as to button its entire length in front; the back part should be made to button from the bottom, to a point about three-eighths of a yard up the skirt. This arrangement does not detract at all from the appearance of an ordinary walking costume. When the wearer wishes to prepare for a drive, she simply loosens two or three of the lower buttons at the front and back and bringing together the two ends of each side, separately, buttons them in this way around each ankle. This gives a full skirt around each ankle, and, when mounted, the dress falls gracefully at each side of the front wheel."

Miss Carrie Augusta Moore, well-known in amusement circles as "The Skatorial Queen," has been riding the bicycle in public in Washington, Boston, and the Western cities, with much success. Her riding is described as finished and graceful, and her costume as neat and modest.

VELOCIPEDE SCHOOLS AND RINKS.

THOSE who have thought the rage for velocipedes would be fleeting and evanescent, have found
themselves much mistaken. Velocipede " Schools,"
" Halls," " Rinks," " Institutes," and " Academies,"
have sprung into existence with mushroom rapidity.
There are scores in our large cities, and one or more in
almost every country town. They secure a patronage
which is not only surprising, as indicating the extent
to which the enthusiasm prevails; but also as showing that the desire to ride is not confined to any
particular age, or to any class of persons. We have
seen astride the bicycle in the same rink, the old and
the young, the fat man and the lean, the doctor, who
does not believe that the fashionable exercise develops
one set of muscles to the detriment of others; the
clergyman, a regular muscular Christian; and the
newsboy who has sold his papers in the cold and
rain to accumulate the funds to make him as much
the privileged character as any nabob. We have
witnessed the lawyer, the tradesman, and the mechanic, spinning with ease and grace. We have
watched the lounger who fringes the edge of society

with his delicate moustache, making his languid attempt; we have seen the artist mount his Pegasus, and the professor of literature, striving with noble persistency to emulate his much envied tutor. There is a marked fascination in the exercise which affects alike the spectators and the participants. Those who come to look, remain to ride; and those, who once bestride "the wheeled Rosinante," refuse to quit until they have tamed the unaccustomed steed.

It is very amusing to watch the eager pupils, going through their novitiate. The beginners mount, struggle, perspire, and tumble in all directions and shapes; and blunders, awkward movements, collisions, and shipwrecks follow each other in constant succession. The more advanced ride with "This one thing I do," manifest upon every feature; and one would suppose, from looking at their compressed lips, knit brows, and fixed eyes, that they felt they were guiding, like Phaëton, the horses of the Sun. The graduates and proficients ride with charming ease, carelessness, and control.

"The early bird catches the worm," is a proverb particularly applicable to those who first started velocipede schools. All the rinks, schools, academies, and "velocipedagogues," do a large business; and their machines pay for themselves in a short time.

The fever is not confined to the Eastern and Middle States, but rages throughout the South and West.

In some of the velocipede riding halls, a charge is made for a series of ten lessons; at others, there is an admittance fee, and a certain price per hour for using the machine. In our cities, we have them to suit all classes and conditions of people. They range from the rinks in common localities, with their sawdust floors, cheap machines, and nominal admission fees, where the "timid toddlers" go it alone, to the schools in the marble blocks, with their French machines and experienced teachers.

As our knowledge increases, our tastes become more luxurious. The plebeian is content with his wagon, but the patrician must have his *coupé*. The beginner asks no better accommodation than is afforded by the New Bedford machine; but one of the "do it gracefuls," or one of the "fancy few" must have spring work, ornamental mountings, bright varnish, and no sawdust under him; else he fails to experience the acme of bicycular enjoyment.

Among the most popular velocipede schools in New York city, are those of the Pearsall Brothers, corner of Broadway and Twenty-second Street; Hanlon Brothers, corner of Broadway and Tenth Street; Calvin Witty, 638 Broadway; Mercer & Monod, No. 3 Williams Street; and Barber & Pendleton, corner of Broadway and Forty-seventh Street.

The Pearsall Brothers formerly occupied prominent. and lucrative positions with Messrs. Gurney & Son, photographers. They foresaw the future popularity of the velocipede, and abandoned photography for velocipeding with immediate success. They opened the first school in New York, and have the names of some five hundred or more pupils on their lists. They have a velocipede ware-room under their hall.

The Hanlon Brothers, well-known as gymnasts, have the reputation of being the best riders in the country. Their hall is the largest in New York, and is furnished with twenty-five first-class machines. They lately gave a "Velocipede Reception and Hop;" and exhibited many graceful and daring feats upon the bicycle; afterwards other gentlemen also gave proof of their skill, among them, Charles A. Dana, Editor of the "New York Sun," who is an expert rider.

The largest and most popular school in Brooklyn is under the direction of Mr. A. C. Burnham. At all these schools, velocipede receptions and exhibitions are of almost nightly occurrence, and create much interest.

Messrs. Crawford & Co., of Philadelphia, have a large school, corner of Eighth and Callowhill Streets, where they use a velocipede of their own construction, in which the rear wheel is used as the guiding wheel.

Messrs. Mercer & Monod, of New York, have a flourishing branch school in Philadelphia.

The Pearsall Brothers have one in Detroit, Mich., and another in Chicago, Ill. The large Zouave Hall in Chicago, under the direction of Geo. D. Miles, has become a noted velocipede academy. The Nicholson pavement, much used in Chicago, is admirably adapted to this kind of propulsion, and the riders soon leave the rinks for the streets. Chicago hails any invention of a fast nature, and the velocipede has already become a practical institution there.

There is no place where the velocipede *furore* has developed more rapidly or to a greater extent than in Boston. There are over twenty schools and rinks in the city; and no less than eleven on Washington Street, between the Old South Church and Chester Square. The first school in Boston was opened by S. T. Derry of the firm of Wm. H. Sargent & Co., at 155 Tremont Street. At this school the course of instruction is thorough and complete, and all pupils graduate experts. Six different sizes of French pattern velocipedes are used, and the scholar is advanced from one to the other, according to progress Though this is a private school, there are the names of hundreds of graduates upon its lists. Mr. Derry is an accomplished teacher. He has several other schools under his charge, and has made arrangements to lease the Skating Rink for the same purpose.

The first public rink opened in Boston, was near

Bowdoin Square (No. 7 Greene Street), and has been deservedly popular. The proprietors have had branch rinks in Cambridgeport, Brighton, and other neighboring towns.

, The fashionable Horticultural Hall was transformed into a first-class velocipede academy for a limited time. This academy was provided with coat rooms, dressing rooms, and other conveniences; and with seats and accommodations for ladies. Tournaments and races here followed each other in rapid succession.

Among the other popular rinks in Boston, are those of Kimball Brothers, 113 Court Street; Walter Brown, 179 Court Street; Horace M. Sargent, Boylston Hall; Macy & Butler, 90 and 92 Tremont Street; at 334 Washington Street; at Arlington Hall; and at Riddle's Carriage Repository, Haymarket Square.

The two best and largest rinks in the United States are to be found at Harvard Square, Cambridge. One of them has twelve thousand square feet of floor, and twenty-five good machines. The other, built by Mr. John C. Stiles, is in the form of an amphitheatre, and has a circular course of a little less than an eighth of a mile in length. Only part of the track is under cover. At night, this rink is brilliantly lighted, and the scene is at once novel and inspiring. Scores of riders rush madly after each other at break-neck speed, round and round the arena. We have seen an expert whirl over the course in seventeen seconds, which is nearly as good time as any recorded abroad, and better than any heretofore made in this country. The students of " Old Harvard " crowd these rinks; the billiard halls and other places of resort are deserted, and all are eager votaries of the fascinating art.

"WHERE SHALL WE RIDE?"

———◆———

But one thing is likely to interfere with the bicycle campaign in our large cities and towns; and that is the difficulty of finding suitable places to ride in. Our latest hobby is already ridden with remarkable fury in the streets, and will continue to be so, by those who make the machine a means of utility. Foot passengers, however, claim the sidewalks as their exclusive rights; and will hardly be pleased to feel in perpetual terror of —

> Bicycles right of them,
> Bicycles left of them,
> Bicycles front of them,
> Rolling and tumbling;

and those who ride for amusement, are anxiously looking for suitable places, where they can do so without annoyance to passers, or being interfered with by them; where they can see and be seen; and where their skill can be admired.

But velocipede tracks are now in preparation. Race-courses will be free to the bicycle, velocipede stables will open in their vicinity, and the proprietors will rapidly line their pockets. All the skating ponds will be metamorphosed into velocipedariums and velocipede rinks. These will make capital exercise grounds, where numberless riders can make their graceful curves to the music of a good band; and where, in hot summer weather, they can be protected from the sun by awnings. The large parks will be open to velocipedestrians.

It has been currently reported that the Commissioners of Central Park, New York, have prohibited the driving of the bicycle there; but the rumor is without foundation. No such interdict will be issued, unless the blooded horses object to the novel machine, by running away. Well-bred horses, whether thorough-bred or not, already manifest no emotion at the sight of the vehicle. Without doubt, the Commissioners will yield gracefully to the public demand.

In New York, a project has been advocated of building an elevated railway, from Harlem to the Battery, to be used only by velocipede riders. On such a railway, thirty feet wide, and with a flooring of hard pine, it would be possible to go from one end of Manhattan Island to the other in about an hour, making allowance for delays, from stoppages and accidents. A good rider, with a clear track, could easily accomplish the distance in half an hour; but, with a well-filled road, progress would necessarily be slower.

In Prospect and Washington Parks, Brooklyn, the bicycle votaries are allowed the same privileges as equestrians. Many of the level streets of that city, with the Nicholson and concrete pavements, furnish a capital surface for the velocipedestrians, and are great resorts. It is even said, that the benign City Fathers propose to bridge the gutters for their accommodation.

The residents of Boston will find good riding grounds, easy of access to the city, on many of the smooth roads of its beautiful suburbs.

Philadelphians can ride the velocipede on their straight, level streets. We know of no place so admirably adapted to the bicycle, as Broad Street, Philadelphia, with its miles of Nicholson pavement.

VELOCIPEDE RACING.

ANOTHER feature of the velocipede campaign, will be races against time, and contests of rival riders. Fast and slow races for money, silver cups, and other prizes, follow each other night after night in most of our rinks. All the race-courses will be used for this purpose. A provision for this sort of sport is in progress, at the Capitoline Ball-ground, Brooklyn, where in May a half-mile track of smooth hard road-way will be ready.

The managers of the Prospect Park Association, of the same place, have made arrangements to signalize their first spring meeting for 1869, with a grand velocipede tournament; at which prizes amounting to $1,500 will be given for the best time, to the winners of a series of races. These races will be governed by a special code of rules, which will include handicapping for weight of machines and riders, diameter of driving wheel, and extent of treadles. There will be first, second, and third prizes for the greatest speed; prizes for the best time made; and prizes for slow riding. This tournament will afford, not only an excellent opportunity for the display of skill in American velocipede riding, but also a fair chance to show off the merits of the different styles of machines. It will create an excitement, and it is anticipated that many thousand people will be present.

The proprietors of Riverside Park, near Boston, also intend to inaugurate a series of bicycle contests on their course during the ensuing summer.

At the last annual meeting of the Housatonic Agricultural Society of Berkshire County, Mass., a vote was passed, offering premiums for bicycle races, at the next exhibition and fair.

Velocipede races are now a feature of the French turf meetings. These are less cruel, and more attractive and exciting, than running horses under whip and spur. In the suburbs of Paris, a race of this kind is especially interesting. The village in which it takes place is in holiday guise; banners flaunt gaily, and eagles, wreaths, and flowers are to be seen in every direction. The mayor is usually present, with a red, white, and blue scarf, his badge of office. The riders wear jockey caps and silk jackets, and at the moment of starting are drawn up abreast. The fair sex mount their chairs, wave their hands, flourish their handkerchiefs, laugh, and scream with delight as their favorites start at the signal. In spite of the exertions of the *gendarmes*, the crowd closes in behind the contestants, who are soon lost to sight. In a few moments, however, distant shouts and cheers announce the return; and the crowd opens, to allow the passage of. the victor, who passes the winning-post amidst great applause.

The fastest time which has thus far been made in France, was one mile in two minutes and fourteen seconds. There is a record also, of two miles having been made in four minutes and fifty-six seconds. This extraordinary speed was attained on a perfect track, with large-wheeled machines.

Among the velocipede wagers which have had place in our newspapers, we mention one or two of the more remarkable. It is said that a Providence pedestrian and rope-walker is to commence, on the first day of June next, the unparalleled feat of pro-

pelling a velocipede of his own manufacture, a distance of three thousand miles in thirty days, averaging one hundred miles per day, for a wager of
$5,000. During the trip, he is to ride the velocipede
one hundred and fifty miles in twenty-four hours,
and one trial only will be allowed.

Two New York gentlemen have wagered $1,500
a side to ride from New York to Chicago. Articles
of agreement have been drawn up and signed with
a forfeit of $250 each.

VELOCIPEDE LITERATURE.

UNTIL very recently, velocipede literature has been confined to some few magazine articles, editorials in · scientific, illustrated, and other newspapers, and various and constant newspaper squibs.

Now, however, the velocipedestrians have a novelty in a paper of their own, which has made its. appearance in New York. It is to be published monthly by Messrs. Pickering & Davis. It is a quarto of eight pages, and is entitled " The Velocipedist." " The object this paper has in view, is to record everything of interest in the velocipede world." It is edited by W. Chester King, late of Athens, Greece, whom Horace Greeley, in the " Tribune " of February 1st, 1869, justly styles a " brilliant and accomplished young litterateur." This young gentleman has distinguished himself, in a marked manner, in various branches of journalism ; and " in velocipede literature he is as far ahead of his contemporaries as, in Virgil, Tityrus tells us, Rome was in advance of other cities. ·

> ' Verum hæc centum alias inter caput extulit urbes
> Quantum lenta solent inter viburna cupressi.' "

VELOCIPATHY.

THE VELOCIPEDE FROM A MEDICAL STAND-POINT.

—◆—

THE vast majority of people are almost wholly responsible for their physical condition. Bodily strength and sound health, like mental accomplishments, are the results of cultivation; and the greater part of mankind can as easily obtain them, as they can acquire a knowledge of Mathematics in school or college.

Let any one place, side by side, the closely confined student or clerk, and the man who has paid special attention to his physical culture. Compare the pale or sallow face, the flat chest, the narrow, stooping shoulders of the former, with the development of the latter, whose vigorous frame defies disease, whose strength gives a consciousness of power that makes him fearless of danger, and who can exult in that greatest earthly possession, exuberant health. These two classes of men will be the fathers of the next generation. The great disparity between them can be obviated by physical training on the part of the former. If not, then, merely as a means of hap-

piness to ourselves, is it not a duty we owe to succeed-
ing generations, that we cultivate these means of
raising man to the summit of his nature, physically
as well as mentally ?

The condition of civilization (if one avoids its
vices), does not weaken bodily vigor, provided the
locomotive system is kept in thorough activity. The
masses should not only have the necessary amount
of exercise in the open air, but a perfect exercise of
every muscle in the body.

A neglect of the powers with which our Creator
has endowed us, is punished by their withdrawal.
Allow the intellect to remain idle and it will become
sluggish. All parts of the human organism not
sufficiently worked, are liable to degenerate; the
nerve force which should guide and govern is allowed to sleep; the muscles become inelastic fibre
of but little vitality. Tie up an arm for months and
it withers away. Let the muscles of our young
men and delicate young ladies remain idle; they
degenerate and atrophy.

"Everything that prolongs human life, amelio-
rates human suffering, elevates and develops the
human frame, is an element of progress; an element
that all true men admire and cherish."

The velocipede is one of the finest inventions of
the nineteenth century. It is a physiologically constructed machine; is an invaluable means of pro-

moting health, and bids fair to emancipate our youth from the common muscular lethargy and debility.

Velocipeding is superior to skating, horseback riding, base-ball, and rowing. While skating is good for the legs, horseback riding for the chest, base-ball and rowing for the legs and arms, the benefit derived from exercise on the velocipede is not local. *It gives a natural exercise and general development to every muscle of the body.* The arms are the first to feel the effect of the exercise, for the pressure of the feet upon the stirrups must be met by a corresponding pressure of the hands on the tiller, necessary to prevent the front wheel from turning. This pressure of the tiller against the hands puts the rider in an upright position, with elbows well back and hands well extended, straightens the stooping shoulders, facilitates respiration, expands the lungs, and develops the chest. No position can be maintained upon the velocipede, inconsistent with ease and elegance of motion, or incompatible with the laws of health.

Some physicians of prominence have pronounced against the velocipede, and one has issued a pronunciamento advising young men to shun it, but the majority of the profession give it their hearty and cordial support. Medical men are among its most eager votaries. One of the best physicians in our country, who makes diseases of the lungs a specialty, rides the bicycle two hours a day, and prescribes it for his patients. He considers it a great preventive of that scourge of our climate, consumption; and a grand aid to the development and improvement of the human body. Many busy men of the profession in New York, Boston, and other large cities, either have their own machines, or ride daily in the schools and rinks. They regard this preparation of Iron (the velocipede), as better than any in their Materia Medica.